CABIN

FEVER

MARIE-FRANCE BOYER

CABIN FEVER

SHEDS AND SHELTERS, HUTS AND HIDEAWAYS

With 134 illustrations, 130 in color

THAMES AND HUDSON

For those who
collect driftwood and
who can tell one
bird's-nest from another.
For those who
love the smell of resin
and hay,
fern and seaweed.

Designed by Michael Tighe

Translated from the French by Esther Selsden

© 1993 Thames and Hudson Ltd, London, and Thames and Hudson SARL Paris

Text © 1993 Marie-France Boyer

First published in the United States of America in 1993 by Thames and Hudson Inc., 500 Fifth Avenue, New York, New York 10110

Library of Congress Catalog Card Number 93–60122

Printed and bound in Singapore

Half-title: Chinese Turkestan,
Dzungarian mountains.
Title pages: fishing cabin,
Gironde, France.
p. 7: corrugated iron beneath the
palm trees of Jamaica.

CONTENTS

Cabins, huts and sheds have always been part of my life. As children, during the long summer holidays on our island in Brittany, we started off by building cabins with floors lined with sweet-smelling fern. As we grew older, we would meet other members of our gang in the tops of fir trees. My father sometimes took me, perched on the frame of his bicycle, to look for oysters in the huts of the local oyster farmers. Black and flat, sunk deep into green and scented mussel beds, with sea-horses pinned to the walls among the yellow oilskins and the black boots, these cabins filled me with alarm: it was rumoured that a pirate was hiding in the area. As an adult I have become familiar with my friends' cabins. I have spent the night in the beach huts of Cotentin at that moment of high tide when the sea just fails to

PREFACE

'I LIVE HERE, RICH AND HAPPY, IN MY HUT — ON NOTHING,' JEAN COCTEAU

wash over the feet of the bed in which one is sleeping. I had a sauna in a bright red beach hut in Finland once, among the wild ducks of the Baltic Ocean. I almost bought a lobster fisherman's hut in Maine. Disused, covered in shingles made silvery by the wash of sea spray and perched on their stilt supports, these old huts soon collapse into ruins. Ten years ago, I moved to Ménilmontant, a working-class district in the East of Paris. Every flat in the block has an allotment, and there was, indeed, one just for me. On the tarred paper roof of the allotment shed, I can hear cats, autumn leaves, rain and hail. I can watch the blackbirds, the 'bleeding heart', the rosebushes. My neighbour, a retired café waiter, repairs his moped on his geranium-filled patch. It's the Paris of Robert Doisneau and Jacques Prévert.

If a cabin is not just a 'diminutive house', what is it? It's neither a shack, nor a lean-to, neither a shed nor a hovel, nor a simple hut, nor an extravagant folly (for a cabin is devoid of all elegant extras). It's not a kiosk or a run-down shanty dwelling, nor a tent, nor exactly a tepee, and yet it's a little of all of these at once. It is a precarious, ephemeral, poetic place, of small dimensions, which blends easily with the natural world. It is closer than one would at first think to a nest, tucked into the fork of a tree, or a crevice in a cliff, towering above the seashore.

It is precisely in a cabin like this that a nineteenth-century walker like Stevenson, in his *Travels with a Donkey in the Cevennes*, dreamt of putting down his bag, to take a nap there, or spend the night, preferably on a heap of dry straw. Yet such

INTRODUCTION

ALL THAT A PERSON NEEDS IN THE WIDE WORLD, UNDER THE STARRY SKY

makeshift dwellings are not destined to last. Constantly threatened by the elements, they offer the human being only temporary shelter, whether by choice or necessity. What is more, they can quickly change from a place of harmony, linked to pleasure and childhood, to a place of poverty, need and sadness.

To choose to live in a cabin is to choose to give up all ties to the consumer society, since any self-respecting cabin has neither water nor electricity and its furniture is limited to a table, a chair, a stove, a kettle, a Lilliputian-sized burner. The only hint of luxury is the collection of pictures stuck onto the walls: a post office calendar, newspaper cuttings, some postcards, some photographs. But though the interior may be basic, the exterior demonstrates an unheard-of-variety of materials. The favourite is wood: logs, branches, storage pallets, builders' timber, railway sleepers, flotsam and jetsam. Then there is corrugated iron for the roof or for the whole construction, with empty petrol-cans to block up the holes. Or cardboard, corrugated paper, tarpaulin, oilcloth, plastic, bits of cars, buses or trams, salvaged doors and windows, earth, clay, mud, cob, palm, fern, broom, gorse, ivy, cane, bamboo, wire mesh, and the lids of metal boilers.

A cave, a tree-trunk, a railway carriage, a builders' shed, pill-box or bunker done up with such materials can serve equally well as a dwelling. All represent a triumph of the imagination. For the cabin comes just after the overcoat, the oilskin, the cape or the shepherd's cloak – it is the human being's minimum shelter in the vast, wide-open world beneath the starry sky.

In search of a sober, natural life, the philosopher Diogenes scorned wealth and material comfort and chose to live barefoot, wrapped in his only coat, in a barrel, from which he held forth cynically and sharply to his fellow men . . .

The cabin also transports us into the magical realms of fairytales – to the Three Little Pigs, Hansel and Gretel, and the dark forests of the brothers Grimm – and also to the adventurous world of Huckleberry Finn and Tom Sawyer.

Today, the cabin has been given a new lease of life by the world of leisure. Luxury travel agents offer weekend breaks to blasé New Yorkers in the simple fishing huts of Vermont and Maine. Similarly escapist dwellings can be hired in Kenya. Adults play at being children, and children play at being adults. But in these artificially simple dwellings there is always something missing, for only a combination of time, luck and imagination can transform a cabin into a place of magic.

For those who still look at the world with an innocent eye, almost all huts – whether for pigs, goats, sheep, hens or for those old donkeys who can survive for as long as sixty or seventy years – have the same power to enchant that the Three Bears' house deep in the forest had for Goldilocks, or the fox's house, built of faggots and turf, had for Beatrix Potter's Jemima Puddleduck.

Wherever it is – high on a mountain, deep in a valley, far off the beaten track, way across a meadow, this small, unassuming building sends out its magic signal. The question that flits across the mind and often remains unanswered is: Who lives there? And our imagination begins to carry us away, so much so that we secretly start to fantasize about setting up home there ... We dream of the

ON THE FARM

EPHEMERAL, ISOLATED, ABANDONED TO THE WEATHER, IT IS OFTEN JUST SALVAGED BITS AND PIECES

sweet smell of fresh straw, of moss, of resin seeping slowly from wood. In Mexico the Terrahuyas Indians of the Sierra Madre build huts on stilts to protect their hens from foxes. From their vantage point, the birds are guaranteed a clear view of the enemy. On Ushant, the islanders put up shelters for ewes about to lamb, on common grazing land out on the moor. These precious and isolated buildings, made from bits of tin and driftwood, have roofs constructed from lumps of earth and roots held together by fishing net weighted with stones.

Some tourists, to the islanders' displeasure, are irresistibly drawn to these huts, sheltered as they are from the prevailing wind, facing the vast sea. Occasionally they give in to their deepest desires and spend the night there.

p. 10: who lives in this French farmworker's hut in the Jura? Is it a witch, or a billy-goat?

A mobile home (*opposite*) is inhabited by goats, chickens, sheep and the children of the house at Toulx Ste Croix in the French Massif Central. In Corsica, a Citroën van is used for a similar purpose, occupied exclusively by sheep.

Left: rusty corrugated iron
at its most splendid in this ancient
sheepfold in Romney Marsh,
in Kent, and (*below*) in a semi-
circular residence which

the RAF bequeathed to cattle
in East Anglia. The Mediterranean
sheepfold (*above*), on the other
hand, is made of flattened tin cans.

Two shelters hollowed out of the cliff for agricultural machinery and for animals on two of the Canary Islands – La Palma and Grand Canary. The cubic structure of stone and iron (*below*) is a protection for sheep.

Opposite: this concoction of planks and string surrounded by cactus happily houses chickens, goats and an old donkey in La Palma, Canary Islands.

In Holland, red, green or black huts serve to house cows or hay (*opposite, top and centre*). The dovecote in Derbyshire (*opposite bottom*) was specially built for a family of homing pigeons. In Corsica (*right*), goats are squatters in a rusty iron structure in which the previous tenants, human beings, made a doorway for their cats.

The residential cabin is a place of extremes. A railway car, a converted bunker, a truck without wheels, chipped, fitted with a chimney that is linked to it in a way as improbable as it is ingenious. A typhoon, a storm or a great freeze will rapidly take care of all of these. This is a habitat subjected to extreme isolation. In Alaska, in Patagonia, in Siberia, basics are shipped in by helicopter and then abandoned on site along with empty tins of sardines and beer cans. A second-rate site arising out of nowhere has drawn a few human souls to work there for a while.

The poorest kind of cabin is to be found most often in developing countries. In Haiti and Madagascar, crossing the shantytowns of Brazil and, indeed, in all of the world's cardboard cities, the sun brings a momentary ray of sunshine, poetry

NO PLACE

ENDURED BY THE POOR, TRANSFORMED BY THE

and ingenuity which will be instantaneously washed away at the first touch of rain. In rural areas of certain African and Asian countries which have not yet been touched by civilization, the leaf or mud hut reminds us of the earliest human beings. The most rudimentary examples include the Zairian farmer's hut in the shelter of his banana tree, the Namibian hunter's mud hut bristling with sticks, the leaf hut of the Amazonian jungle and the central Asian yurt which is made of skin and tree branches and set into a vast expanse of landscape.

For the festival of Succoth, the Jewish 'festival of tabernacles' five days after Yom Kippur, many people still build their own huts on balconies or in gardens, roofed with branches and leaves (with the roof left partly open to the elements). This shelter symbolizes the fragile, temporary dwellings in which the Israelites lived while they wandered in the wilderness during the Exodus.

If the cabin has a mythological quality for some people, it is very much a symbol of identity for others. 'To rediscover his identity', as he put it, Thierry Thiboideau, who is now a shop-fitter and lives in a perfectly normal flat, spent fifteen years in a collapsible cube some 3 metres by 1.5 metres square. 'During the 1980s, I lived in a commune. I invented the 'module' – some planks and a few nuts and bolts – for myself and a few friends. With a mattress and two or three shelves, I reconstructed the space in which I wished to live. I was guaranteed minimum dignity within the group but was able to think of myself as an isolated individual.'

LIKE HOME

RICH, IT GOES FROM ONE EXTREME TO ANOTHER

In Canada, the Mohawk Indians, forced to inhabit a reservation far from their ruined forest, dissociate themselves from the prefabricated, anonymous cabins provided by the government by decorating their doors with moose antlers.

Tramps, also, sometimes choose cabins as a statement of freedom. Though they could go and live in a hostel, they prefer to set up home in the open air under a bridge or facing the ocean, with a mean bed which may be meagre, but which they have selected themselves, just as they chose for companions their old, pet dogs. Certain affluent members of our fin-de-siècle society also opt for a degree of privation, but suffer it in countries where the sun shines. The American decorator, Stewart Church, for example, has settled in Morocco. This designer of night-

An old German bunker facing the
Channel in Normandy, a few
hundred yards outside a village,
adapts well to a new use.

clubs, shops and Gulf magnates' palaces, has retired to a life in the hills fifty kilometres from Tangier with a friend, twenty dogs, a few donkeys and a variety of cats. There is neither electricity nor a telephone, but Stewart has granted himself two luxuries: he gets his water from a natural spring, at great cost, and he has had a small, golden monument built at some distance from his house, a kind of sophisticated kiosk in which he can sit and watch the sunrise and the sunset.

Robinson Crusoe, who is often cited as an example, didn't actually have a choice. For him, real life was vested in all the objects of civilization that he unloaded from his boat just before it sank. Many of the thoughts that occupied his mind related to improving his quality of life by accumulating material goods. One imagines that,

'AT WHAT MOMENT DOES A PLACE REALLY BECOME YOURS?

IS IT WHEN YOU HAVE PINNED UP ON THE WALL AN OLD POSTCARD OF CARPACCIO'S

***DREAM OF SAINT URSULA?'* GEORGES PEREC**

had he been alive in the twentieth century, and had he been able to reenter civilization, he would have made a wonderful durable goods consumer.

Nevertheless, he summarized perfectly the kind of problems the nascent cabin – or 'my castle', as he liked to call it – poses. 'I consulted several things in my situation which I found would be proper for me; 1st, Health, and fresh water, . . . 2dly, Shelter from the heat of the sun. 3dly, Security from ravenous creatures, whether man or beast. 4thly, A view to the sea; that if God sent any ship in sight, I might not lose any advantage for my deliverance.' But the kind of people who choose this natural, get-away-from-it-all lifestyle nowadays, although no doubt complete with their fax and their favourite laptop computer, choose it for good.

As sophisticated as one of those owned by the American couturier Ralph Lauren, this seaside cottage, in Cap Ferret, southwest France, is roofed with 18th-

century tiles from St Emilion. Here the elegant man of the world can play the peasant among the pines and the yuccas, accompanied by his wife and seven children.

In Montana, USA, this tiny second home (*below*) recalls the 'cabane au Canada' of which Line Renaud sang in 1950. By contrast, it was to

preserve his own cultural identity that this Mohawk Indian (*right*) put the deer antlers over the gimcrack wooden hut where he lives a sad life on a Canadian reservation.

These stalls (*opposite top*) and caravans, called 'Diogenes' after the philosopher's barrel (*opposite, centre and far left*), are brought by helicopter in separate pieces to Siberia for technicians and workers to live in. They then remain for ever in the immense landscape of Vortuka. Some of the workers find it a good idea to give them a lagging of fur (*opposite, bottom right*).

Right: in Hastings, in the south of England, this freight waggon, augmented by a chimney and a neat little garden, will never get back on the rails.

Overleaf: at Urumai, on the celestial lake of Xinjiang, China, the nomads raise and lower their tents of animal skins stretched on wooden poles, in order to follow their flocks.

In the Orange Free State, South Africa, the decoration by women of the exterior of their mud huts (*left and top right*) with painting to drive away evil spirits is becoming less and less common. The decoration on the Haitian hut (*bottom*), on the other hand, celebrates the joie-de-vivre of a country that has little else to celebrate.

Centre right: a railway carriage in Norfolk displays the humour that seems to be expected in such situations: 'Linga Longa'.

Overleaf: at Bahia, in Brazil, the inhabitants throw their rubbish down from huts perched on poles. It is a shanty-town packed with children, but every house has that miracle of technology – the colour TV set.

The Himbas of Purros, famous rhinoceros-hunters of Namibia, build huts of earth moulded on tree-branches. *Far right*: a holiday bungalow in the West Indies; a Chinese tent, the rolled-up bundles of cloth for travelling giving it a special atmosphere (see also pp 30-31); and a hut in Zaire with mud walls.

Difficult to locate, the cabin set deep within the forest is primarily a hunter's lair. In order to trick its prey it must disappear into the natural world. A covering of broom, fern or pine may render it as invisible as a bird's plumage. In Les Landes, near Bordeaux, 'the dove catcher' can be found at the tops of pine trees, linked to the ground by a ladder camouflaged by a tunnel of greenery. In this watchtower, reigning over the forest, men come often to escape from home, be together, and imitate birdsong. But though the hunter in his cabin may be surrounded by a benevolent natural world, the walker in the woods fears meeting the inhabitant from the depths of the forest,

DEEP IN

A SECRET PLACE, KNOWN ONLY TO CHILDREN,

whether this be a prowler, a poacher

or a witch from 'Hansel and Gretel'.

Though of course it could just be a

rather magical, benign old woman, with

an owl perched on her shoulder and

squirrels and dormice as her eiderdowns.

The make-believe world of such

places is very closely related to that

of childhood. A universe in which one can

pretend to be an adult, far from parental eyes, is a place of initiation into the sounds and the cold of night, into solitude and, of course, into sexuality: there is no better place to reveal the secrets of young bodies brushing furtively against each other, or to play at doctors and nurses.

On the island of Mayotte, it is customary for all boys on attaining the age of puberty to build a 'banga' in the woods away from the village. There they have the right to sleep and mess about without any interference from the community. 'Scouts' too, benefit from this freedom of spirit if not of body, and remain great cabin technicians. Thanks to their practical skills and their unlimited knowledge of knots, they can build cabins between two or more tree trunks and among the

THE WOODS

HUNTERS, WITCHES, SMUGGLERS AND FREEDOM FIGHTERS

thinnest of branches. For the treehouse cabin also has its devoted followers.

This way of life, which Tarzan borrowed from the chimpanzee in the jungle, was taken up by the French at the beginning of the 20th century. They invented a popular pleasure garden to the South of Paris, called 'Robinson', which became very well-known. You could dine in the treetops, having already danced under them and, most importantly, you could laugh and

Preceding page: visitors in the 19th century climbed up to platforms in this tree at Montibo in Piedmont, Italy, to take the air and enjoy views over the countryside.

Left: this tree-house at Pila, in Engadine, Switzerland, belongs to the children of the local charcutier who is noted for his skill in making the smoked meat characteristic of the Grisons. *Right*: a similar house in Lithuania. In both countries the children desert their houses during the winter, returning to their secret life when the summer holiday arrives.

drink with the 'looser women' who appeared on Saturday evenings, half-hidden among the branches. This idea may seem a bit outdated now, but .it has been taken up with much success in the enormous magnolia tree at the Mutiny Hotel in Florida's Coconut Grove, which can shelter as many as sixty guests.

A permanent tree dwelling has been created by an eccentric Swiss citizen in India, though he does come down from time to time, which is more than could be said for the Barone Rampante (the 'climbing baron'), described by Italo Calvino. He ascended into a tree at the age of fifteen only to descend, finally, as a corpse.

Which is all less improbable than you might think. The official news agency of Nigeria, NAN, recently reported the case of a forty-five-year-old Mhwelis citizen

MONTAIGNE TELLS US HOW HE CLIMBED AN ITALIAN TREE COMPLETE WITH PLATFORMS AND A THOUSAND FOUNTAINS, ALL GIVEN OVER TO THE PLEASURES OF VISITORS SCATTERED AMONG THE FOLIAGE

called Michael Dilamo, who climbed up into a tree in 1987 and then simply refused to come down again, despite the prayers and pleadings of his two wives and his nine children. He would occasionally, as a great favour, descend to one of the lower branches to take some nourishment.

It is in trunks hollowed out over the course of the years that certain fairies prefer to live. Catholics sometimes set up statues of the Virgin or various saints inside them. In Normandy, in the trunk of a yew that people say is five hundred years old, you can even find an extravagant little gothic chapel that looks enchanted: does it set up some form of communicative link with the elves at the centre of the earth in order to draw terrestrial powers from its depths?

When she was thirteen, the future Queen Victoria climbed the 600-year-old lime tree in the garden of Pitchford Hall, Shropshire, to watch the fox-hunt from the little Tudor tree-house with Gothic windows. Built in 1692, this must be the oldest tree-house in the world.

The Landes, southwest
France. Can one not imagine this
hide of sweet-smelling
pine as the setting for a François

Mauriac novel, with lovers
engaged in an illicit affair slipping
secret messages to each other
through gaps in the planks?

Opposite top left: at Robinson, a popular rendezvous to the south of Paris, visitors around 1900 could enjoy a Saturday evening dance and then retire to the tree-tops where their meal would be hoisted up to them. *Next to it*: a 'folly' recommended in a garden manual of 1859. *Centre, left and right*: the house of an eccentric Swiss in India who, like Italo Calvino's 'climbing baron', settled down to life in the tree above his wife's restaurant. *Above left*: at Sadat, on the island of Mayotte, near Madagascar, adolescent boys build themselves these 'bangas', where they have the right to sow their wild oats before marriage.

At water-level for ducks (*below left*) and high above the trees for wood pigeons (*opposite left, below*), the hunters of the Landes, in France, first build and then disguise these strange structures which also allow them to regress to a primitive way of life that is tolerated by society.

Following 4 pages: a Dutch painter's country retreat.

These and preceding 2 pages: for thirty years, winter and summer, a middle-aged youth has arrived by bicycle to take up quarters in an isolated country retreat in Holland.

He is a painter. He brings with him his violin, his paints, and some bread and cheese. Here he takes refuge from the hubbub of an excessively consumerist society.

Turn-of-the-century bathing huts come immediately to mind, even those pulled by horses to the water's edge so that scantily clad ladies could slide modestly into the brine. Not much bigger these days, beach huts are rented by the season, particularly in England, where they are built and decorated with a freedom of style that pushes local tolerance to its limits. In them, one may take tea or have a picnic lunch or play cards sheltered from the wind, with the doors wide open and a clear view out to the wide expanse of horizon . . . A whole ritual way of life contributes to the enjoyment derived from these small constructions, which can also give rise to despair, jealousy, passion. As soon as you get further South, preferably 'in the shade of a palm-tree', the hut-on-the-water's-edge becomes synonymous with

BY THE WATER

CREATED FOR WORKING FISHERMEN, IT WHISPERS NOW OF FREEDOM, SUN AND PLEASURE

lazing in the sun, the life of the wild, nudity, bronzed torsos and the inevitable fishing for a catch that will be grilled and eaten on site. In the Canary Islands, the remote village of Garasia consists of colonies of precarious shelters, heavily padlocked, nestled into the cliffs. On Sundays the men arrive early to fish. The women, all in black, with their knitting and their children, come down in the evening by way of a path that is as perilous as it is pebbly. At sunset, in front of the cabins which overhang the void, they cook fish in great cauldrons. They dine. It's a kind of happiness that can never be properly expressed in words alone.

Basic, workmanlike fishermen's huts are found on rivers, on lakes, on the most humble of ponds. In Canada and in the United States, in Maine, Connecticut or

Vermont, cabins like these are rented out to chic holiday-makers, who arrive from New York, Boston and Montreal to fish for salmon, watch blue herons, eat blueberries, and sleep in narrow, iron beds with 'Indian' quilts, hanging up their trappers' jackets above their 'Bean boots': this is the life of the wild!

In Scotland, right on the edge of the peninsula that makes up their estate, the Kenniel family have constructed a shelter that faces the sea and is firmly attached to the ground by a network of steel roping. When the weather begins to look stormy, certain family members, in a grand ceremonial procession, loaded with thermos flasks and provisions, leave the eighteenth-century, oak-covered house and cover the few miles of land that lead to the ocean. There they watch the wind

IN A SAUNA, THE PLEASURE COMES FROM MOVING OUT OF A HUMID DARKNESS, INFUSED WITH THE SCENT OF SMOKE, RESIN AND BIRCH LEAVES, INTO THE ICY WATERS OF A BALTIC LAKE

rise up and the sea roar and break against the islands of Islay and Jura. It will be an incredible night. Tomorrow, they will go and bid the seals good morning.

On the Scandinavian coast, at the far end of a wooden pontoon, which juts out into the rushes, on islands of rounded boulders glowing like seals, the Swedes and the Finns construct tiny saunas, painted bright red. These little cabins, such as the one that Armi Ratia, Marimekko's founder, owned on the Baltic Sea, offer the opportunity to move from the wet, hot, shadowy darkness, infused with the scent of smoke, resin and birch leaves, into glacial waters . . . This regeneration of body and spirit, through their relation to nature, will never be better expressed than in one of these small, red, magical, wooden boxes, hidden in the birch trees.

p. 52: it was on this volcanic rock, some distance from Las Palmas, Grand Canary, that Christopher Columbus put ashore to repair the rudder of his ship *Punta* in 1492. Now fishermen store their oars, nets, bait and outboard motors.

p. 55: this hut (*top*), held together with metal bands, and equipped with a primus-stove and four bunks, is used by the Kenniel family, in Ard Patrick in Argyll, Scotland, to watch the storms round the islands of Islay and Jura. *Below*: on a stony beach in southern England, the coastguard's office is a wooden cabin covered with pitch.

'I live here, rich and happy, in my hut – on nothing,' wrote Cocteau early this century: three such poetic summer residences for Sunday fishermen – at Hastings (*opposite* and *overleaf*) and Walberswick (*left*).

It is the old sailor's love for a vessel that can no longer put to sea – rather than any practical justification – that accounts for

these upturned boats on Holy Island, Northumberland (*opposite*), in Lithuania (*left*) and on Isle d'Yeu in France (*above*).

Dream holidays. In Thailand, on Koh Phiphi island (*centre two pictures*), and in Kiwayu in Kenya (*top right and opposite*), there are 'Robinson Crusoe' beach hotels that combine the luxurious and the hippy, with palm-trees, grilled fish, papaya, coconuts and suntan guaranteed. The Tahitian floating house (*bottom right*), on the other hand, is the setting for traditional customs that were still flourishing in the 1950s.

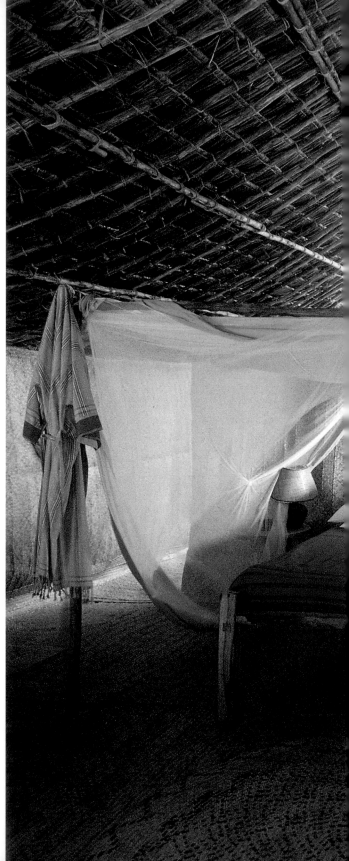

In France, in the Gironde (*left and opposite top*) and the Loire estuary (*opposite below*), the marshy ground makes it necessary to build huts on stilts, where the men who come to fish for plaice might be tempted to camp out, as in a tent.

A humble French village (*right*) and a grand château in Holland – Twickel (*opposite*) – show similar calm river banks bordered with irises and similar shelters for favourite boats.

The painted window in the Dutch farm building is false, but the knitted socks made to wear inside traditional wooden clogs are genuine.

This is the most civilized. Here you can store bicycles, folding chairs, bits of wood. The retired gardener, having reached an incredibly advanced age, can, despite limited resources, regain a certain freedom here, and dream up secret projects with the help of a thousand oddments – pots of paint, wire, string, cuttings . . . And there are also hutches, henhouses, vague constructions on which tiny creatures perch, creatures that are being reared 'in principle' to be eaten.

In some wooded areas, all these tangled cabins form a complex, muddled mass, which brings to mind a multiplicity of thrilling activities, which will help you to put up with life's woes, the passing of time and the tyranny of work. It was in this spirit that a number of large industrial corporations in the nineteenth century

GARDEN REFUGE

LOVED BY THE ELDERLY AND THE GARDENER, IT ENCOURAGES ESCAPISM AND CREATIVITY

invented the allotment, or working man's garden, a patchwork of plots the size of handkerchiefs, each one provided with an individual shed. These collective entities exist to this day, in suburbs, in certain working-class, urban districts and all along railway lines. Today they also attract less traditional tenants, who attempt to cultivate elegant lawns and grow organic tomatoes.

In the evening, everyone locks up his or her hut and the old gentlemen who like reading in the sun and doing their crosswords sometimes leave a dictionary lying permanently on the tiny dresser, protected by a piece of lino. These huts guarantee tranquillity, without whose sheltering presence one could not remain so far from home for a whole day.

In the little allotment that she has rented for forty years, Maria Hofker has made herself a hut out of old materials. Over ninety years of age, she goes out every day to tend her roses (Louise Odier, Mme Isaac Pereire, New Dawn, Souvenir de la Malmaison), her Japanese anemones, her phlox, her poppies, her rows of delphinium and her flowering shrubs, and then to draw

them and paint them in watercolour. In her retreat she has a gas heater to make herself tea, hats, umbrellas, a campstool, a watering can, an old easel, the remains of a dry cake in a box and a few enamelled dishes.

Overleaf: in a seaside village on the Scottish island of Islay, a former worker in a whisky distillery protects his plants from the frost.

Near Chiswick Bridge in London: how to live close to nature and grow leeks in your own back yard (*right and below right*). To the north of London (*opposite top left*) and in Scotland (*opposite top right*), one has the pleasure – as in a boat – of arranging around one everything one needs to enjoy life. In the Allier area of France (*opposite below left*) this woman does not need to take off her apron in order to pick a salad in ten minutes. In England, the aptly named organic gardener Bob Flowerdew has a hut at the end of his garden (*below left*). In Holland, Anton Shlepers has set up a stuffed goose among the honesty drying in his garden shed (*opposite, below right*).

In the mountains of the Lyonnais, in France, the oxblood metal of the shed, repainted every year, sets off the lupins' pastel shades.

Opposite: huts for a variety of uses: for the children of the French painter Gérard Garouste (*far left*); for doves (*top left*); and (*remaining pictures*) for a Dutch musician who has no legal right to build a broom-shed . . . When he goes to the kiosk (*top right*) to have tea, he calls it 'going to Russia', because of the onion dome.

Above left: a Swiss hut in an exemplary vegetable garden and, in an Alsatian garden (*below*), a chalet room built in 1900 as a guest bedroom.

Overleaf: at Twickel, in Holland, a forgotten shed slowly falling to pieces by a mysterious pond.

The huts that cast their shadow on the edge of the road from Rockfield in Jamaica (*near left*), or the painter Judy MacMillan's hut on the hills of St Ann, Jamaica (*opposite*), are exotic examples of their genre. *Left, top and bottom*: at Cascais, in Portugal, in a public garden heavy with rare perfumes, and beside the interminable straight lines of a Uruguayan highway.

The professional cabin is a seasonal item, depending on the popularity of a particular geographical location. It establishes itself there, it opens, it closes, and then it disappears again according to habit and custom. Shut up in winter, it becomes nostalgic and absurd. Repainted in the spring, looking brand new, it offers the prospect of happy holiday memories and suntanned children. But in August it is overwhelmed, overrun by an all-consuming, idle crowd.

The cabin in question sells chips, mussels, ice-cream, sausages, kebabs, candy-floss, sandwiches, fruit, pancakes or waffles, according to where it has sprung up – on the North Sea, the Atlantic or the Mediterranean; in the Alps, for skiers and hikers; in Switzerland, in Hyde Park or in the park at St Cloud. Or, in Alabama, in

CABINS A

JUST THE PLACE FOR AN EXTEMPORE SNACK, HERE TODAY, GONE

Australia, in certain popular summer destinations, it can expand into a mini-grocery store or gas station for a season or two, before being abandoned to its fate.

More ephemeral still, liable to turn up in the street one morning and then vanish without trace the next, are the sewermen's cabins, in direct communication with the town entrails. The workman's hut, a solid cube brought to any site, wherever it may be, is a temporary habitat. Workmen change inside its sheltering walls, exchanging their smart clothes for working overalls. They heat up their billy-cans of low-cost lunch; sometimes they even sleep there.

Somewhat similar are the three 'boxes' of around 2 by 4 square metres which are occupied by the members of the stone-cutting team which is restoring the lighthouse at Cordouan, a Renaissance masterpiece, twenty kilometres out at sea, near Bordeaux. These three orange cubes were hoisted in pieces right up to the enormous, circular King's Chamber. You may discover them, windowless, equipped with a basic bed, side by side on the multi-coloured marble floor. And yet these craftsmen do have a choice: they could have stayed in the lodgings of the lighthouse keepers. But they say they've got used to it now, this return to the lifestyle of the snail, the hermit crab and the whelk.

Joined directly to water are the coastguards' cabins, those of lobster fishermen and those of oyster-farmers. That of the Russian washerwoman, at the end of a jetty on the Volga, becomes redundant and closes up shop when the ice becomes too hard

T WORK

TOMORROW – BUT THE ONLY ONE OF ITS KIND IN BUSINESS

to crack. On fine days, these women leave their tubs and their soap in the cabins, put the baby's pram into the cabin's sheltering shade, and wash on their knees, straight from the river, with coloured scarves fastened tightly round their heads. Cabins of resin-gatherers and basket-cane collectors (those dwindling professions!) may be found in the vicinity of forests. They are constructed between four living trees, hazel and chestnut, the same trees on which the men will begin work – making baskets, fencing or chairs – when the sap shows them to be ready.

The writer, who can, after all, work anywhere, with just pen and paper, typewriter or computer, often chooses a cabin close to home. 'A room of your own' is more often than not 'a room with a view' – usually of the writer's own family, complete with domestic noises and temptations. In order to write in peace, the writer must break away, spending his or her days in a shed, like Dylan Thomas, or in a garden hut, like Henry James, Roald Dahl, Virginia Woolf or Bernard Shaw.

Gustave Mahler wrote a large part of his oeuvre in a wooden shelter. On the island of Huva-Oa, in the Marquesas Islands, Gauguin lived in a 'fare', made from nailed-down planks, carpeted with bamboo lathing and covered with a roof of woven coconut leaves. It was both a studio and a living space. The painter carved the words 'House of Pleasure' on one of the three panels which framed the door. It was there that Gauguin, after having painted, written, sculpted and loved far more than his fair share, died sadly and ignominiously in 1903.

HERE ONE CAN BUY FRENCH FRIES, MUSSELS, HOT DOGS, CANDY FLOSS, TOFFEE APPLES, WAFFLES AND PANCAKES, BALLOONS AND SHELLS . . . THEN IT CLOSES UNTIL NEXT YEAR

Thirty years ago, another painter, this time a Dutchman, transported a studio cabin into the woods, onto land lent to him by an old peasant woman, far away from any town. He lived there with his violin, his tobacco, his pastels and his charcoal, cooking meals in an ancient frying pan on a 20-cm-square burner. With time, his cabin became furnished with all sorts of oddments gathered in from the fields: feathers, fossils, horseshoes, strangely misshapen tree knots – a collection as delightful as it is strange, never seen and certainly never purchased.

Just as isolated, but much more frightening, looming suddenly up at you, are the smugglers' haunts and those of the trappers, which remain the most difficult to photograph, or even to locate.

Left: like all of its kind: busy in summer, fast asleep in winter, a waffle kiosk by the sea in Binic,

Brittany. *Above*: the ever-active coastguard station at Aldeburgh, Suffolk.

A garage somewhere in central France which once serviced postwar Panhards and Vedettes, now stares out blindly under a wig of young vines which will soon smother it altogether.

Dylan Thomas's blue shed not far from the boathouse at Laugharne (*opposite, top left and right*) in Wales, where he lived; the wooden hut at the bottom of Virginia Woolf's garden (*opposite below right*) at Rodmell, Sussex; my own little refurbished caravan under a maple tree in Ménilmontant, Paris (*opposite, bottom left*) and the pink metal shed (*right*) of the Australian writer Jose de la Vega disappearing under *Pandora pandorana* – all four are scholarly and strangely similar.

A hut on the steps of the Madeleine
in Paris. In it workmen can change
their clothes and heat their food.
Tomorrow it will probably be gone.

On the flanks of Etna, in Sicily (*top left*), and amid an immense cornfield in Champagne, France (*opposite top*), maintenance huts serve to keep working tools. The caretaker of a chalet estate on the Thames estuary uses a small cabin as his base (*below left*). The huts of lobster fishermen in Stonington, Maine (*centre left and opposite below*), might have come out of a painting by Andrew Wyeth. Here they take the lobsters directly from the boats and wash, weigh and measure them, as well as keeping their lockers, boots, oilskins and outboard motors ready for the next fishing voyage. To amuse themselves, they often decorate the huts with old red buoys which seem to light up in the fog.

These huts could almost swap places – one (*right*) for the groundsman who looks after the sports field at Montacute, Somerset; one for the plate-layer at Tenterden, Kent (*far right above*); and a boathouse at the end of a landing stage in Sweden.

Sheds in business: all these huts are the centres of selling operations – coffins, at the end of a highway in Kenya (*opposite top*); groceries and snacks for travellers in an isolated spot of the Everglades, Florida (*opposite below*); shellfish, coral and starfish for tourists at Montego Bay, Jamaica (*above right*); flowers, fruit and vegetables in East Anglia, with a box for customers to put their money in (*below right*); and a barbecue-hut at the end of the ski-run that joins Sils-Maria to Majola in Engadine, Switzerland (*below far right*).

A cabman's shelter in Chelsea, London, where taxi-drivers can rest, socialize and make tea (*below*);

and (*right*) a shed for garden furniture in a public square in Mulhouse, France.

'Nature calls' is one euphemism, 'going to the bottom of the garden' is another. Outside privies have not disappeared quite so absolutely as one might think. Guy and Geneviève Gibaud, who live in France, in the Creuse countryside, are market gardeners. They inherited an outside toilet which had just collapsed, and they proceeded to build another, on the same site and identical in every way. Young, modern, cultured *Le Monde* readers, they do not think they could ever get used to anything else. The Gibaud's instructions for building an outside loo are strict and run as follows: "The construction must be spacious enough to be able to move around inside. It will be built entirely of chestnut wood, and that includes the seat, with openwork walls so that you can look out

NATURE CALLS
OUT OF DATE OR UP TO DATE? BACK TO NATURE, OR THE HEIGHT OF SOPHISTICATION?

without other people being able to look in. The view should be pleasant. It should be at some distance from the house, reachable without inconvenience with the help of a torch, and with one or two nails on which to hang clothes.' The Gibauds decline to use salvaged china 'bowls', just as they refuse to use cement breeze-block which could insulate them from the world outside.

Are they behind the times or ahead of them? They are, it seems, far removed from the puritanism of the nineteenth century and in line with the recent rediscovery of the body and of nature. They agree to a surprising extent with the words of Tanuzaki, a Japanese philosopher who praised the outside lavatory in his book *In Praise of Shadows*. He did, however, identify two obvious problems: the distance involved, particularly at night, and the risk, in winter, of catching a cold; but what's all that compared to the advantages the experience offers?

'Every time I go to a monastery in Kyoto or Nara and someone shows me the path that leads to the outside toilets, built in the manner of days gone by, in semi-darkness and yet meticulously clean, I feel intensely that rare quality of Japanese architecture . . . Always slightly away from the main building, the toilets are situated in the shelter of a copse, in which the scent of green leaves and moss greets you . . . And in provinicial oriental buildings, narrow, long openings have been specially put in at ground level, mainly to allow detritus to be swept out, but in such a way as to enable you to hear, close up, the soothing noise of raindrops

'OUR ANCESTORS, WHO ALWAYS EXPRESSED THEMSELVES IN POETRY, SUCCEEDED, PARADOXICALLY, IN TRANSMUTING INTO A PLACE OF THE UTMOST GOOD TASTE A SITE WHICH . . . SHOULD HAVE BEEN THE MOST SORDID'

which, falling from the edge of the guttering or from the leaves of trees, splash onto the feet of the stone lanterns and dampen the moss growing on the flagstones before they drain away into the floor . . . Our ancestors, who always expressed themselves in poetry, succeeded, paradoxically, in transmuting into a place of the utmost good taste a site which, by definition, should have been the most sordid and, in partnership with nature, have made it blur into a network of delicately associated images. Compared to the attitudes of people in the West who consider themselves to be liberals and yet have decided that the whole concept is unsavoury and that no public mention should be made of it, our attitudes are wiser, for we are the ones who have brought the idea to the heights of sophistication!'

p. 102: outdoor (indeed, without-door) privy in the Camargue, facing the Rhone delta with its spectacular panorama of pink flamingoes. It belongs to the owner of a caravan permanently parked a short distance away.

Left: lavatory and bathroom with shower, in a hostel for walkers in Katmandu.

Two examples of a smallest room
with a view, both private and
conveniently separated from the
residences they serve – one

(*above*), in Montana, overlooks an
immense mountain landscape: the
other (*right*), built of shingles, in
Connecticut, looks out over a lake.

Left: a wooden lavatory suspended over the marshes of the Baie de Somme, at the end of a meadow which functions as a garden. *Below*: this privy, at Creuse in the Massif Central, made of layered chestnut,

overlooks the proprietor's vegetable garden. Another (*opposite*), set amid birch and pine on a Swedish estate only a few yards from the house, seems to pride itself on its tasteful decoration.

ACKNOWLEDGMENTS

For their help and enthusiasm, I thank in particular: R. Beaufre,

M. F. Bouchaud, V. Breton, J. V. Brown, J. Dirand, A. Garde, F. Gilles,

J. P. Godeaut, J. Darblay, F. Halard, J. Hecktermann, M. Heuff,

M. Hogg, F. Huguier, T. Jeanson, F. Martinet, J. Powell-Tuck, D. and B. Wirth: and all

the other photographers who kindly lent their work.

My thanks also go to: S. Howell, E. Morin, B. Saalburg, Norbert X. Slavik,

I. Terets Chen Ko, Michael Tighe, A. J. Walter.

Above: a chapel in a yew tree, Normandy, France

PHOTO ACKNOWLEDGMENTS

Roland Beaufre 37*t*

Henry Bourne, *World of Interiors*, 43

M. F. Boyer 16*t*, 17, 83*t*, 90*bl*,
96–97, 108*r*

Véronique Breton 47*t*

Luc Choquer, *Marie Claire* 26–27

Tim Daly 33*c*, 94*b*

Jérôme Darblay 41, 78*l*, 99*br*,
106–107, 109

Gilles de Chabaneix 16*b*, 52

Jacques Dirand 18*t*, 40, 61*l*, 61*r*, 65*t*,
76–77, 88–89, endpaper *cb*

David Ferris 60

Anne Garde 1, 30–31, 37*c*, 44–45, 45*r*,
46*cl*, 46*br*, 47*b*, 64, endpaper *rc*

Denis Gilbert 32–33, 33*t*

François Gilles 55*t*, 100*l*

Jean Pierre Godeaut 2–3, 22–23,
25*l*, 25*r*, 34–35, 62*t*, 62–63, 65*b*, 79*b*,
92–93, 100–101

Groupe Huit 33*b*

François Halard 102

Jerry Harpur 74*bl*

Joan Hecktermann 98*t*

Marijke Heuff 10, 18*c*, 48–49, 50, 50–51,
55*b*, 67, 68, 70*l*, 70*r*, 71*l*, 71*r*, 75*br*,
78*tl*, 79*t*, 80–81, 90*br*, 94*t*, 95*t*, 105

Min Hogg 75*tl*, 83*br*

Françoise Huguier 28*t*, 28*bl*, 28*cr*, 28*br*,
72–73, 75*tr*

Thibault Jeanson 13, 15*br*, 16*l* and
endpaper, 19, 26*l*, 66, 78*tr*, 78*b*, 106*l*,
endpaper: right hand page *br*

Cookie Kinkead 7, 82–83, 83*c* and
endpaper, 99*t*, endpaper: left hand
page *tl*, *bl*

Clare Lambert 12

Bernard Marie Lauté 87*l*

Francis Martinet 108*l*

Gideon Mendel, *Observer* magazine
36–37

Paul Montecalvo 94*c*, 95*b*

Julian Powell-Tuck 14–15, 56, 57, 58–59,
87*r*, endpaper *rt*

George Seper, *Vogue* Australia 91

Alan Shepherd 90*tl*, 90*tr*

J. F. Teaule 46*bl*

Michael Tighe 15*t*, 18*b*, 62*c*, 62*cb*, 99*bl*

John Vere Brown 29

Alison J. Walter 97*t*

Frank Watson 74*t*, 74*br*

Didier Wirth 37*br*, 97*br*

World of Interiors 38–39, 46*tl*, 46*tr*

Debra Zuckermann 98*b*, 98*br*